The Humans Lost in Time

Evolution Unraveled, Volume 7

Vaishali Alapati

Published by Vaishali Alapati, 2022.

THE HUMANS LOST IN TIME

First edition. November 28, 2022.

ISBN: 979-8215898413

Written by Vaishali Alapati.

Also by Vaishali Alapati

Evolution Unraveled
History of Evolutionary Thought: Part 1
History of Evolutionary Thought: Part 2
"Dark-DNA"
Epigenetics 101
The Full History of Evolutionary Thought
The Humans Lost in Time

Table of Contents

Part 1

Intro

At first, the Latin word evolution meant the unrolling of a scroll. This gives the flavor of the inevitable recitation of a story or message. The story has already been composed; all that is needed is to "read off" the message in a consistent fashion from beginning to end. However, there isn't a beginning and an end.

To put it simply, in biology, evolution is the idea that all species on Earth evolve from other pre-existing organisms and their characteristics change over several generations. People from all over the world tell tales of how the world began. All current people who live in traditional (such as hunter-gatherer tribes, nations, or chiefdoms) or state-level societies adhere to a specific set of origin-related concepts.

Any ideas that fall outside the realm of science, however, are considered creation myths and are an aspect of a culture's religion. Creation myths are mystical, cultural, or spiritual stories that explain the roots of humanity, earth, nature, and the universe. One of the reasons why creation stories are universal is that all cultures and civilizations have the same basic questions about life, such as "Where did the universe and the earth come from?", and "Why do we humans exist?". Because it is human nature to ponder the unknown and search for answers. All the creation stories we know today stem from these very questions.

For example, Genesis, the creation myth of both Judaism and Christianity, contains two origin stories, both of which are accepted as the creation of the world by the beliefs of modern Judaism, Christianity, and Islam faiths. In the first, God says, "Let there be light," and light appears. In six days God creates the sky, heaven, land, plants, the sun, moon, stars, animals, and humans.

On the first and second days, God created the sky, light, and heavens. On the third day, the soil and vegetation were created. On the fourth day, the sun, moon, and stars. The fifth is the aquatic and avian creatures. Finally on the sixth, land-based wildlife and humankind. He created fish in the seas, birds in the air, and all kinds of flora and fauna on the land. God had gifted these creatures with gills to breathe, wings to fly, eyes to see, etc. To all, he says, "Be fruitful and multiply," which they do. All the handiwork of an omniscient God. On the seventh day, God rests and ponders his handiwork. The second story is of the well-known Adam and Eve.

Some of these legends have found their place in history and long eclipsed the civilizations that first gave them a voice. Some of us hold to the ethics and morals that were illustrated in the folklore and epics of people who died centuries before us, who spoke languages we will never understand, experienced things we will never experience, and who lived in lands we will never touch.

The passage of time, the concept of birth, and the vision of an all-knowing creator are among the common threads across creation stories, although some are quite unusual. So what if creation stories of contrary cultures share similar aspects? In particular, a theme of many fables in numerous cultures, including those of Greece, Egypt, and Mesopotamia, presents primeval water as the lone element that existed in the beginning. Many philosophers have developed their ideas based on this recurring theme.

That the fabric of the universe was built from primeval water. The "qi" or mist, which represents the divine power that embodies the cosmic force governing matter, time, and space, is one exception to this rule. It was the core first element in Chinese cosmology.

According to Chinese historical texts, this energy changes at the moment of creation, breaking into dual aspects of male and female, Yin and Yang, hard and soft matter, and other binary components. Which leads to the Chinese origin story. Several legends begin with the cracking of a cosmic egg, including a Chinese one.

A primordial cosmic egg floated within the infinite void containing chaos, a mixture of forces of yin and yang. Over time, the interplay between multiple elements and energies eventually conceived a primal being—a shaggy, horned giant named Pan-Gu. Pan-Gu (pan goo) slept and matured for 18,000 years. One day, he mysteriously awoke. When he opened his eyes, all he could see was a heavy veil of darkness. He strained his ears, but all he could hear was the unnerving silence. He was deeply disturbed by his somber environment.

After eons of incubation, Pan Gu grew agitated and conjured a magical ax, swung it down, and gave the egg a mighty chop. The egg split into two with a thunderous crack. He separated chaos into the many opposites, including Earth and sky, he set the sun, moon, stars, and planets into place, divided the seas, and chiseled valleys and mountains. The denser piece, (Yin) of the egg drifted downwards, forming the earth. The lighter piece. (Yang) rose to form the sky. Pan-gu feared the parts might re-form, so he stood in the center, his head in the clouds, and his feet firmly planted in the soil.

He stretched together with the Earth and Heavens as they both rose by 10 feet every day. He grew 10 feet per day for another 18,000 years, the sky was higher and the earth was thicker. Pan Gu loomed between them like a pillar 30,000 miles in height, so they would never again connect. When Pan Gu died, his parts transformed into facets of the universe. His skull became the crest of the sky, his voice became the rolling thunder, his breath the breeze and clouds. His right eye glowed into the Moon, while his left eye blazed into the Sun. His flesh and limbs turned into five huge mountains, and his blood formed rivers. His muscles turned into lush meadows and his veins became roads. The innumerable stars in the sky popped out of his hair and beard, and trees and flowers sprouted from his skin. His teeth and nails hardened into precious metals. His bone marrow turned into jade and pearls. His sweat flowed like a sweet dew and a gentle shower that balanced all life on earth. Some say that the parasite that plagued his body became an ancestor of mankind.

Others say that When the goddess Nuwa felt isolated, she fashioned men from Yellow River clay and sculpted them into human figures in a similar way to how a ceramic craftsman would make a sculpture. After creating these creatures for a while, Nu Wa ran out of energy and realized that if she created each by hand, she would not be able to inhabit the planet. So she took the rope, pulled it out of the mud, and then lifted it. She threw mud in all directions and all the drops that hit the ground split into several humans. The people sculpted by Nu Wa became the wealthiest and most influential people in the world, and the people she rushed into making became sick and poor.

There are countless legends that reflect the above as creation stories. Some more well-known and some less. No matter how widely accepted a creation story is, it always attempts to answer the same questions: where did we and everything we see come from, and why? One of the things we can trust to answer this question is the idea of evolution.

In order to bring clarity and context to our story, it's important to understand all the philosophies and beliefs that precede the modern theory of evolution. We've built our society, advanced in technology, and our ability to observe and adapt many theories through simple research.

Consider this a snapshot of evolutionary philosophy, highlighting some of the most notable evolutionary thoughts, from antiquity to the Age of Enlightenment to the present.

The beginning of evolutionary thought can be traced back to Anaximander, an Ancient Greek philosopher who lived from (610 BC to 546 BC). He believed that life began in the waters, and that evolution flowed from there. He also concluded that man evolved from another creature, such as a fish, and evolved into a creature similar to fish. Human infants cannot live without long-term care, while certain animals, like fish, can survive on their own right after birth. Anaximander speculated that humankind's ancestors were sea creatures who migrated to dry land.

Anaximander wasn't the only ancient Greek philosopher investigating the origins of humans. Empedocles, who lived from (490 B.C to 430 B.C), held that dismembered organs, born out of the Earth, came together to design bizarre creatures. He imagined arms without shoulders, cattle with human heads, and many more terrifying creatures. He could have been influenced by previous tales of Greek mythical creatures like centaurs, gorgons, sphinxes, and chimeras that appeared to be "stitched together" out of multiple animal pieces.

However, because of the Church's influence, evolutionary ideas were thereafter prevented from spreading and posing a threat to the doctrine of special creation for roughly fifteen centuries. So that explains the significant jump in the timeline we're about to experience. Now we've come to the Age of Enlightenment aka the 18th century.

In the 18th century, the Age of Enlightenment was a cultural movement that revolutionized European philosophy, research, and ethos. The quest for truth and knowledge, and the emphasis on logic and reason rather than mysticism and superstition, was central to the Enlightenment, which challenged traditional beliefs and pursued modernity.

Despite the fact that the sense of progress and development was the core of the eighteenth-century enlightenment, it did not lead to a significant theory of evolution. When Georges-Louis Leclerc, Comte de Buffon, a French naturalist, published his Natural History of Animals, a 44-volume encyclopedia of all known facts of the natural world, he made another major step toward modern evolutionary theory. He first proposed the possibility that all animals were descended or evolved from a common ancestor or prototype living in the "land of origin", which is the perfect place for them, a place he imagined was Europe.

What is Degeneration?

Buffon described the similarities found in the bones of the limbs of very different animals. For example, he noticed that the dog's leg had bones similar to those found in seal fins, even though the two structures were used in very different ways. Being expelled from their ancestral homes would lead to improper climate and/or degeneration from perfect prototypes, though he didn't believe in mutations. According to Buffon, degeneration was the most widespread and extreme of the creatures farthest from their ancestral homes. In Essence, it's a de-evolutionary thought. The notion that evolution is directional and that the species can eventually return to a seemingly simple form is called de-evolution, or backward evolution. However, evolution has not been determined in advance. Over time, the animals gradually moved away from the key prototype by degrees.

One might use examples of de-evolution using birds as a reference. The evolutionary innovation that granted modern birds the upper hand over dinosaurs was their far shorter incubation periods, but it came at the sacrifice of their teeth. Due to the complexity of evolution, there is often a myriad of overlapping arguments for why specific traits are adaptive. The source of the bird's beak, not the teeth, is one such unsolved mystery. Theropod dinosaurs, including some of these ferocious carnivorous creatures with jaws full of jagged teeth, such as the Velociraptor and Tyrannosaurus Rex, are the ancestors of modern birds. They evolved from extinct creatures like Archaeopteryx, the link between dinosaurs and birds. Thankfully, even the most vicious birds of prey of today lack teeth, yet experts are unsure of why birds lost their dental care. As per one explanation, teeth ultimately gave way to beaks in order to minimize weight for flight. However, 2014 research published in Science counters this hypothesis by showing that tooth loss and nascent beak formation happened at about the same time.

DNA from the crypt is a powerful tool for unlocking secrets of evolutionary history," Mark Springer, a professor of biology at the University of California, Riverside, and one of the study's lead researchers, said in a statement.

Following the cataclysmic extinction at the end of the Cretaceous period 66 million years ago, ecological adaptations, including the evolution of beaks, are considered to have spurred the explosive diversity of birds. Speaking of birds, penguins can also serve as a model of alleged de-evolution. The issue is that categorizing such as "devolution" assumes, falsely, that flying is an endpoint that evolution is working towards.

Flight was convenient and permitted ancestral penguins to enhance their reproductive performance, thus it was selected. After the large dinosaurs were extinct, penguin ancestors quickly lost their capacity to fly. With fossils dating to around 60 million years ago, the oldest known penguin was already a flightless swimmer with thin wings. Modern penguins still have feathers, wing bones, and a jutting breastbone for wing muscle attachments, which are identifiable hallmarks of their avian ancestry. However, flying was not favorable to penguins, and it was beneficial to be plump, therefore selection operated against aviation, and adaptations for surviving in frigid climates emerged. Penguins naturally adapted to their new climate, not "de-evolving," as a result. Flight was no longer an advantage, so they evolved accordingly.

Back to Buffon, he suggested organic change, that creatures manifest from organic compounds by spontaneous generation, for context, spontaneous generation is the supposed method by which life spontaneously arises from inanimate matter. For example, rations of cheese and bread wrapped in rags and left in a hidden corner were thought to generate mice because mice were eventually discovered in the cloth, even though this was because it was an ideal food source for the mice. Worms were also suspected to emerge from the combinations of soil and water, while maggots happened to come from rotting meat. This was later proven false. He suggested the potential for productive hybrids of organic molecules as there are flora and fauna. Despite the fact that he did not provide a unified framework for these changes.

Erasmus Darwin

Regarding evolution, various philosophers and scientists from the age of enlightenment, famously Erasmus Darwin, an 18th-century English physician, proposed different aspects of what would eventually become evolution. His philosophy is found in Zoonomia, his two volume medical textbook which aims to establish laws that explain the mysterious classifications, sexual selection, organic life, competition, etc. that surround animals. It was a text studded with thoughts on natural history, and human life and origins. His thoughts on the diversity of life and evolution are also published in The Loves of Plants. Erasmus Darwin was not as famous as his grandson Charles Darwin, although he laid much of the groundwork for evolutionary principles in poetry, through his ambitious work Zoonomia, where he wrote:

"Would it be too bold to imagine, that in the great length of time, since the earth began to exist, perhaps millions of years...that all warm-blooded animals have arisen from one living filament...?".

He discusses ideas that his grandson elaborates on years later, the idea of common descent from one living filament, or one ancestor as he previously wrote.

Taking the reader on a journey through the evolution of mankind, through millennia, through heroic couplets and vivid imagery: this was the experience of Darwin's final poem, The Temple of Nature, an epic about the history of the Universe.

To quote an extract from his poem:
"Organic life beneath the shoreless waves
Was born and nurs'd in Ocean's pearly caves;
First forms minute, unseen by spheric glass,

Move on the mud, or pierce the watery mass;
These, as successive generations bloom,
New powers acquire, and larger limbs assume;
Whence countless groups of vegetation spring,
And breathing realms of fin and feet and wing."

John Ray & Carolus Linneaus

The Englishman John Ray was the first scientist to conduct a comprehensive study of the natural world in the contemporary sense (1627 - 1705). Ray attended the grammar school in Braintree and was the son of the Black Notley village blacksmith. He matriculated at St. Catherine's Hall, one of the colleges at the University of Cambridge, in 1644 with the aid of a fund that had been created in trust to profit needy students there, then switched to Trinity College in 1646. Ray had come to Cambridge at the ideal time for one with his talents, for he found a circle of friends with whom he explored anatomical and chemical curricula. He achieved superior learning advancement as well, earning his bachelor's degree in 1648 and being elected to a Trinity fellowship the following year. For the subsequent 13 years, he resided modestly in his collegiate cloister. Ray was an exemplary student who, in contrast to the custom at the time, opted against taking holy orders after earning his degree from Cambridge (largely due to the social and religious upheavals associated with the Civil War, but also because of his own personal beliefs).

With the Restoration, Ray's long streak of good luck came to an end. He was a staunch Puritan and refused to take the oath required by the Act of Uniformity, despite the fact that he was never an enthusiastic partisan. After being forced to resign from his fellowship at the university, Ray was supported in creating his catalogs of the living world by his friend Francis Willughby (1635–1672). Willughby shared Ray's interests in science. His first work, an inventory of plants growing in the Cambridge area, was published in 1660, marking the start of his professional career. Ray started to go across the rest of Britain when he had finished studying the Cambridge region. A pivotal moment in his life transpired on a voyage to Wales and Cornwall in 1662 with the naturalist Francis Willughby. Willughby and Ray decided to explore the entire natural history of all living things, with Willughby handling the animal kingdom and Ray handling the plant kingdom.

The first fruit of the agreement, a journey across Europe from 1663 to 1666, markedly expanded Ray's mastery of flora and fauna. The two companions started working on their allotted mission once they got back to England. Ray created a Catalogus Plantarum Angliae (also known as a "Catalog of English Plants") in 1670. When Willughby unexpectedly passed away in 1672, Ray assumed the responsibility of completing Willughby's half of their project. Despite having made at least as many contributions as Willughby, Ray published F. Willughbeii... Ornithologia (The Ornithology of F. Willughby...) in 1676 under Willughby's name. Additionally, Ray authored F. Willughbeii... de Historia Piscium (1685; "History of Fish "), whose publication was financed by the Royal Society, of which Ray was a fellow.

However, Ray never stopped working on his botany studies. His contribution to classification, the Methodus Plantarum Nova, which he first published in 1682 and subsequently modified in 1703 as the Methodus Plantarum Emendata, insisted on the taxonomic relevance of the contrasts between monocotyledons and dicotyledons, plants whose seeds germinate with one leaf and those with two, respectively. The foundation of species as the elite rate of taxonomy is Ray's enduring legacy to botany. He erected his masterpiece, the Historia Plantarum, which was issued in three enormous volumes between 1686 and 1704, on the Methodus. He was asked to write an entire system of nature after the first two volumes. In order to achieve this, he created brief summary of British and European plants, a Synopsis of Methodica Avium et Piscium (1693; "Synopsis of Quadrupeds"), and a Synopsis of Methodica Animalium Quadrupedum et Serpentini Generis (1713; "Synopsis of Birds and Fish"), each of which was published posthumously. A significant portion of his final decade was devoted to an innovative study of insects, which was eventually published as Historia Insectorum.

In conclusion, Ray had a powerful fascination with plants, and he designed an early classification scheme for them centered on physiology and anatomy. In this study, Ray developed the contemporary idea of a species, using it as the basic unit of taxonomy by noting that organisms of one species do not interbreed with members of another. Ray contributed significantly to the taxonomy's architecture in all of this activity. He made an effort to build his classification systems on all structural elements, including interior anatomy, as opposed to just one criterion. He firmly developed the class of mammals by emphasizing the importance of the heart and lungs, and he grouped insects based on whether they performed metamorphoses or not.

In addition, Ray examined fossils, realizing that they were once-living organisms, and he was puzzled by the inconsistencies between the biblical account of creation and the evidence of change and extinction he encountered in his fossil collection. He was a devout Christian who, like many scholars of his era, rejected the idea that the Earth was ancient, primordial, and forever evolving.

Before the reign of Darwin, a genuinely natural system of taxonomy could not be realized, although Ray's system came closer to that vision than the blatantly artificial systems of his contemporaries. He was one of the remarkable early pioneers who made Carolus Linnaeus' contributions in the century that followed, imaginable.

Another innovative 18th-century thinker was Carolus Linnaeus, a Swedish botanist, who designed the hierarchical structure of the plant and animal taxonomy that is still used today. He is often called the "father of taxonomy". He has a deep passion for nature and an admiration for the natural world. To sum up his inner motivation for system design, natural science would reveal the Divine Order of God's creation, and the naturalist's goal would be to build a "natural classification" to indicate this Order in the universe. Thus, his impulses were primarily religious, which led him to natural theology. Linnaeus had strong religious convictions as he grew up in a household that valued religion and nature. He believed that since God made the world, one could learn about God's wisdom by looking at the world he had created.

Like Buffon, Erasmus Darwin and Carolus Linnaeus, there are many scholars and philosophers who decorate the history of evolutionary thought, but French naturalist Jean Baptist Lamarck proposed the first theory of evolution in the early 19th century.

What is Lamarckism?

Lamarckism is the concept that an organism could transfer physical features developed during its lifetime to its offspring. The traits acquired during the life of an organism, or "acquired traits," are at the heart of Lamarckism. Organs that are frequently used by living things continue to develop, but rarely used qualities will be lost in future generations. But how do you get those acquired traits? Lamarck's most famous example of this was the giraffe.

Picture ancestral giraffes: these creatures roughly mimic contemporary giraffes, but lack their signature lengthy necks, which stretch to about half the length they are now. According to Lamarckism, the necks of ancient giraffes lengthened over time because they stretched for the tree leaves. As a result, the next generation of giraffes was born with elongated necks that stretched even further.

Lamarck also proposed, like in the giraffe example, that a blacksmith builds muscle in his arms and passes it on to his kids. He argued that evolution was a constant process of enhancing intricacy and perfection. In summary, he argued that these changes were induced by changes in behavior and environment, which resulted in a shift in the use and disuse of target organs. His idea was mocked and ridiculed at the time, and it did not hold up in light of contemporary knowledge. However, Lamarck did contribute to putting thoughts of evolution on the map and stimulating future research.

Charles Darwin

However, the current evolutionary theory wasn't written until Charles Darwin, Erasmus Darwin's grandson, published On the Origin of Species.

In 1831, Charles Darwin received the opportunity of a lifetime: to join the HMS Beagle as the ship's naturalist to travel around the world. Charles Darwin set sail on the HMS Beagle on a voyage around the world that lasted until October 1836, just a few months after graduating from college. In September 1853, Charles Darwin and the crew of the Beagle reached the Galapagos Islands, where they had the chance to catalog the plants and animals. When Darwin first landed on the islands, he was a creationist. His five-week trip to these extraordinary islands catalyzed a revolutionary theory. Over the course of nearly five years at sea, the Beagle studied the coast of South America and took longitudinal measurements all over the globe. Darwin later called the Beagle voyage "by far the most important event in my life," saying it "determined my whole career." Darwin, then 22 years old and fresh out of school, had his sights set on becoming a clergyman when he went off on his own. By the time he landed back in London, he had become a renowned naturalist and was well known for the extraordinary collections he had sent ahead. He had also grown from a promising observer into a probing theorist. The Beagle voyage would provide Darwin with a centuries-worth of experiences to ponder—and the seeds of a theory he would cultivate for the rest of his life.

He went from Tahiti to New Zealand to Africa, and for much of the 5-year voyage, he scouted the Southern American coast. Darwin encountered several rare and exotic birds and animals while exploring San Cristóbal, the outermost island in the Galapagos archipelago. He questioned how life initially came to these islands. He collected thousands of specimens, which he crated, shipped home for further research, and filled dozens of notebooks with precise observations of the animals, plants, and geology. "The natural history of these islands is eminently curious, and well deserves attention," he further observed. "Most of the organic productions are aboriginal creations, found nowhere else." Nonetheless, all of the species had a striking resemblance to those found on the American continent.

The animals that fascinated Darwin the most became the ones he is most well known for: finches on the Galapagos Islands, which varied drastically from island to island. He discovered that each finch species had a unique beak shape based on the opportunity for foraging on the island. Finches that ate large nuts had powerful beaks for splitting open the nuts. Finches that ate small nuts and seeds had blunt beaks which were used to fracture nuts and seeds. Darwin observed that fruit-eating finches had parrot-like beaks, but insect-eating finches, such as the warbler finch, had slender, piercing bills. Or the woodpecker finches, who made use of twigs and cacti, with their elongated bills. Darwin reasoned that the novel Galápagos finches must have started as accidental colonists from Central and South America who gradually drifted to remote islands and diverged from their ancestral stocks after landing in the Galapagos.

After visiting each island, he proposed that the finches evolved independently, adapting to local conditions. This might have resulted in the evolution of unique species on each island. The Galapagos finches are perhaps the most famous example of evolution and are closely tied to Darwin and his expedition. But how could this happen? How did they evolve autonomously? If this theory was accurate, why was it accurate? What approach could explain how each finch species generated modifications or features that made it well-suited to its natural environment? To answer these questions, Darwin introduced the powerful concept of "natural selection".

A publication establishing the role of natural selection in directing the trajectory of evolution, and developing evolutionary ideas, *On the Origin of Species*, was published by Darwin in 1859. Over the course of the twenty years prior, the radical theories revealed in the Origin had been formulated largely in secrecy. Despite being created in a haste in just thirteen months, the new book was the fruit of an exceptional degree of inquiry and careful review. There was a great deal of excitement in the public following the publication of The Origin of Species. As audiences reviewed and discussed the book, notables of all stripes—scientists, politicians, clergymen, and others—defended or disparaged Darwin's theories. The publication was written in an accessible, non-mathematical language for any bright, educated person to consume. From the beginning, it pressed society as a whole to re-think the origin of the universe and all species, as well as the universally held vision of divine creation. To put it lightly, it was controversial and inspired a lot of debate on philosophical, theological, and scientific grounds. The English biologist T.H. Huxley, sometimes known as "Darwin's bulldog," was the most renowned player in the conflicts that ensued soon after the book's release. He defended the idea of evolution in a number of papers and public forums using witty, erudite, and occasionally mordant language. It is clear that during the 1860s and beyond, evolution through natural selection was a hot topic in society salons. But there were also major scientific disagreements, first in Britain, then on the Continent, and lastly in the United States. It required humankind to realize that we are one among many in the 'great family' of living and once-living things: vegetation, insects, animals, birds, and fish, as well as the minerals and rocks that bear the symbols and legacies of earlier life.

The Copernican revolution, which had started in the 16th and 17th centuries under the leadership of people such as Nicolaus Copernicus, Galileo, and Isaac Newton, approached its second and final stage under Darwin. Darwin must be regarded as an important imaginative revolutionary who launched this era in the cultural history of humanity. Modern science was born with the Copernican revolution. Traditional conceptions about the essence of the cosmos were questioned by astronomical and physical discoveries. The seasons and rains that help crops grow, as well as catastrophic storms and other vagaries of the weather, came to be realized as facets of natural processes. The revolutions of the celestial bodies were now clarified by simple laws that also accounted for the motion of projectiles on Earth. Earth was no longer perceived as the center of the universe but as a single planet revolving around one of the innumerable stars. People were capable of abandoning the popular notion of special creation thanks to his groundbreaking theory of evolution by natural selection. Moreover, it empowered them to design their ideas purely on scientific principles. Darwin was able to establish his theory over a great deal of antagonism and cynicism, which made it possible for it to transcend the science of its time.

Natural Selection

Individuals in a population will naturally have properties that allow them to survive and procreate based on environmental conditions, predation, nutrition, and so on. Individuals with adaptive traits are more likely to survive and breed, equipping them with more children than their counterparts in successive generations since the traits make them increasingly efficient at survival and reproduction.

Consider the example of the peppered moth, a moth that can naturally be both dark-colored and light-colored. In the 1800s, a mystery emerged in Great Britain. The Industrial Revolution, as it's known now, was taking place in England at that time. Construction crews were building factories that operated on coal for fuel. The skies were camouflaged by busy factories' ominous black smoke from coal and firewood burning. Tree trunks were charred and exposed to smokey pollutants. The moths were clearly impacted by all this. Victorian scientists soon noticed a change in peppered moths as well. Due to the finite lifespan of moths, this evolution based on natural selection took place fairly quickly. The result is a fresh all-black variation that differs from the original salt and pepper colors. The Betularia carbonaria, or "charcoal" variant, has become its nickname. The older version was known as the Typica.

During most of the Industrial Revolution, the same oily soot that clung to the worker's skin also dyed tree trunks black. The old-fashioned, light-colored peppered moths were clearly identifiable by birds as they had settled onto charcoal-colored tree trunks. Thus, the melanic form of the moth was better camouflaged and more likely to survive and produce offspring, while the paler form became more apparent to predators. As a result, for generations, black moths in towns and villages began to overwhelm their pale counterparts.

Some people believed that the parents changed color in the same vein that the larvae could mimic the twig's colors. Others believed that the chemicals and toxins in the smoke caused the shadows of the moths. Instead, their new dark cousin blended in. As a result, those carbonaria had a lower likelihood of being eaten. Unsurprisingly, as the population of their dark counterparts grew, the number of light-colored moths began to decline. By 1970, almost all peppered moths in certain heavily polluted areas had turned black. Things began to change in the second half of the 20th century.

With the implementation of protective measures to reduce air pollution, trees grew healthier and lichen growth increased as air quality improved. Companies were no longer able to diffuse as many sooty emissions into the atmosphere. Once more, the black varieties of the Peppered Moths were easier to locate than the common fair ones.

Currently, Typica moths have regained their dominance and Carbonaria moths are becoming scarce. The moths did not turn black from contamination. It just gave a cloaking advantage to any moths that held the genetic mutation that turned their wings black. So, it's been shown that natural selection operates in both directions, always rewarding the moth in which is most harmonious with its ecological conditions.

These favorable qualities quickly become more prevalent in the population, and favorable traits are passed down through the generations through the process of natural selection. It was essentially "survival of the fittest". In the case of the Galapagos finches, if they shared a common ancestor, they should all appear and behave similarly. However, exposure to diverse islands and ecosystems would result in different adaptive traits, different body sizes, beak shapes, colors, and the eventual development into many unique species. There must already be diversity within the species for natural selection to occur, so there needs to be heritable variation caused by random mutations. These two terms refer to the fact that new heritable traits are initially produced by random mutations. Genetic variation provides the reference point required for natural selection. In order for natural selection to act on a feature, there must already be changes and the ability to carry those changes to offspring.

Many believe that this kind of event has happened innumerably in the history of life on Earth. Charles Darwin claimed that all existing creatures descended from a small number of primitive species. He compared the evolution of life to a big tree. The trunk symbolizes some of those common roots, and the large network of branches and twigs reflects the tremendous complexity of life that has evolved from it. It sparked several further discoveries in evolutionary science and is now recognized as one of the multiple mechanisms of evolutionary change (which also include genetic drift, mutation, gene flow, etc.).

One of the things that Darwin fails to explain is the modern concept of heredity, which later filled the gaps in his theory of natural selection. The main flaws of Darwin's evolutionary theory lay in gaps in the explanations of the genesis of species and the mechanisms of evolution. Natural selection maintains that genetic differences between individuals rise in nature, demonstrating that distinct variations are desirable given the circumstances, and as a result, organisms are able to generate more surviving offspring. Darwin was unable to clarify how these mutations first appeared or how they were passed onto offspring and successive generations.

Mendelian Genetics

The missing link in Darwin's argument was provided by Mendelian genetics. Gregor Mendel was a lifelong generation theorist. He started young on the Moravian farm he was raised on. Due to his family's modest economic means, Mendel struggled to pay for his education as a young man. In an initiative to boost the produce and robustness of fruit trees by selective breeding and grafting, his father collaborated with the local priest. Up to 3,000 of the resultant trees were distributed among the local farms. His professor suggested Mendel to the Brno Augustinian monks who prized research, knowledge, and education. The monastery was a cultural and intellectual hub. His professor considered him a strong contender because of his prodigy in both mathematics and physics. Before Mendel was welcomed into the order on September 7, 1843, he had no notion of becoming a monk.

He took over the monastery's research garden from his mentor, Friar Klacel, in 1846, while teaching natural science, physics, and botany. Klacel had been studying heritability and variation in pea plants. Peas were another area of fascination for Gregor Mendel, likely as an influence of his mentor. This choice was vital to his eventual success. Pea plants have easily identifiable traits, can self-fertilize, and are easily prevented from cross-fertilization. They were his model plants. A model system is an organism that enables scientists to delve into a certain scientific question, such as how traits are passed down through families. Researchers can establish broad concepts that apply to other, more complex creatures or biological systems, like humans, by researching model systems. Over the years, he ultimately tended to 10,000 pea plants. Mendel did not anticipate carrying out the first rigorously planned and executed genetics studies. His aim was to produce hybrid pea plants and then analyze the outcomes. His discoveries inspired additional research, which resulted in strikingly prescient insights. Mendel pioneered the concepts of heredity, coined the phrases dominant and recessive, and was the first to apply statistical techniques to assess and determine hereditary information by simply measuring the peas and meticulously recording his observations.

Mendel crossed tall plants with short plants, and all of the offspring were tall, never of medium height. He then bred those offspring together, and three of the four children they had were tall, but only one was. Mendel was fully aware of what this implied. Height was passed down in particles we now call genes. Depending on the random gene combination a plant inherited, it could be either short or tall. Therefore, an adaptive mutation could be diffused across a species without ever being wiped out. Small mutations are the cornerstone of Darwin's theory of natural selection, which may remain true.

Mendel put out three primary principles about inheritance.

Typically, Mendel's Laws of Heredity are phrased as follows:

1) The Law of Segregation: A gene pair determines each inherited characteristic. So that each sex cell only contains one of a pair of parental genes, parental genes are randomly allocated among the sex cells.

2) The Law of Independent Assortment: Different trait genes are organized in separate groups so that the inheritance of one trait is independent of the inheritance of another.

3) The Dominance Rule: Organisms having the dominant form of a gene express other alternative forms.

Before Mendel's findings, the general consensus was that parent-offspring traits were mixed. However, Mendel found that when he cross-pollinated two of his purebred plant lines, rather than producing two hybrids, the progeny resembled either of the parents. Mendel, for instance, did not produce offspring with semi-wrinkled seeds when he crossed plants with wrinkled seeds to those with smooth seeds.

Mendel conducted two lectures on his experiment at the Brno Natural Science Society, and the following year, the findings of his labor were published in their journal, entitled "Experiments on Plant Hybrids." Mendel's work was commonly disregarded by his scientific colleagues during his lifetime, despite the fact that the data was published in the "Proceedings of the Brunn Society for the Study of Natural Sciences" in 1866. However, Mendel did little to publicize his work, and the scant references to it at the time suggested that most of it were misinterpreted.

After his death, his work was virtually shelved for nearly 30 years when it made a revival in the 20th century. Finally, The "modern synthesis" typically refers to the early to mid-20th century composition of evolutionary theory that aimed to explain the origin of biodiversity by melding the classical Darwinian theory of selection with a more recent population-focused insight of Mendelian genetics. To put it simply, the Modern Synthesis describes the fusion of Mendelian genetics with Darwinian evolution that resulted in a holistic, singular theory of evolution. It is sometimes referred to as the Neo-Darwinian theory. It is also characterized as the Neo-Darwinian theory. In the 1930s and 1940s, a number of now-famous evolutionary biologists devised the Modern Synthesis.

The Modern Synthesis transformed how evolution and evolutionary processes were perceived in numerous ways. It proposed a fresh view of evolution that would emphasize the genetic basis of evolution as "changes in allele frequencies within populations." The evolution of allele frequencies has been shaped by four forces, which have been identified.

These include natural selection, mutation pressure, gene flow, and random genetic drift. Natural selection is the sole evolutionary mechanism that results in creatures being more acclimated to their environments because it offers the best-adapted creatures the greatest chance of survival. Random fluctuations in allele frequencies within a population are alluded to as genetic drift. In tiny populations, it is incredibly potent. Gene flow reflects changes in allele frequency brought on by people moving into and out of a community. All genetic diversity originates from mutation, variations in the DNA sequences brought on by errors in replication or other factors. Mutation is a weak evolutionary force, but it is vital.

The Modern Synthesis understood that most mutations are unfavorable (have a negative effect) and that fortunate mutations typically have a minor phenotypic impact. Natural selection can enable advantageous mutations to become a part of the population. Therefore, changes in species happen gradually as a result of the accumulation of minor alterations. Large differences between species are a result of slow change over prolonged time periods. The evolution of reproductive isolation, frequently during a time of allopatry, in which two populations are isolated from one another, leads to speciation (the formation of new species).

The Modern Synthesis and the more classical Darwinian theory of evolution diverge in a plethora of ways. First, it is agreed that mechanisms of evolution other than natural selection play critical roles. Second, the Modern Synthesis is successful in explicating genetic variation's permanence, a challenge for Charles Darwin. Blending inheritance, which maintained that kids were the genetic intermediaries (in-between versions) of their two parents, was the most widely accepted genetic theory at the time of Darwin. As Darwin accurately discovered, mixing inheritance would advance the genetic diversity within a population to a point where natural selection would have nothing to work with. This issue is resolved by using Gregor Mendel's particulate theory of inheritance, in which the alleles of a gene remain distinct rather than mingling.

The Modern Synthesis involved a number of key individuals. The notion was based on the population genetics research of Sewall Wright and R. A. Fisher. Numerous features of the idea were supported by Theodosius Dobzhansky's considerable research on wildlife populations of the fruit fly Drosophila. The biological species concept and models for speciation were developed by Ernst Mayr. Paleontological data was included in the Modern Synthesis theory with the aid of George Gaylord Simpson. G. Ledyard Stebbins contributed tenets (principles) based on his botanical work.

Part-2

We've already covered the full history of evolutionary thought, so today we're taking a tour through time, and shedding light on the lost humans of our ancient pasts. This second part's goal is to inform you about the puzzles, cutting-edge breakthroughs, and the past of human evolution. In the last few volumes, we explored the progress that led to the present theory of evolution and several theories on how humans evolved. We only briefly discussed human evolution. Many people have attempted to and continue to attempt to unravel the secrets of human evolution, from the epic creation stories to the Ancient Greek philosophers. So let's start from a place we're comfortable with.

Intro

Think of history, what's the first thing that comes to mind? Just take a moment to pause and think. Does your mind wander to the pyramids of Ancient Egypt, The Rise and Fall of the Aztec Civilization, The Discovery of the Americas, or maybe the Industrial Revolution.

Today's world owes an immense debt to the mighty empires and great cities of ancient history. Their inventions and ideas enabled the advancement of human society and laid the foundation for modern life. But is it possible to dig a little deeper for the full story? What happened before history? The grand story of humanity starts on Earth. The history of humans is not a clean, linear process with clear beginnings and conclusions.

It constantly adds new chapters and rewrites itself. Some of the greatest evidence showing how Homo sapiens developed is shown in this evolutionary timeline. All leading up to the world we live in today with other fascinating creatures, tigers, parrots, jellyfish etc. This amazing tale explores the most profound mysteries of humankind, which merges findings from the archeological record with the most recent genetic research to find out who we are, where we came from, and what the future may hold for our existence. It is the story of a family tree whose tangled and knotted branches span several epochs and continents. Let this story immerse us into the saga of human evolution, commencing with the earliest traces of our hominid ancestors in Africa and continuing through waves of human expansion across the continents to the emergence of agriculture and the explosive growth of the world's population. Many hominin specimens belong not in our solid line of ancestry but on side branches of humankind—evolutionary experiments that ended in extinction. We now realize that the human saga is far more nuanced than the scholars of yore could have ever envisioned. There is no single missing piece binding apes and humans, and there is no smooth drumbeat march forward towards a preordained destiny, shattering the neat clichés of our prehistory. Our tale is blurred, jumbled, and random, but it is one that needs to be told. There are myriad questions unanswered, evolutionary dead ends, and a spirited cast of ancient ancestors of early hominins. This does not imply that scientists have everything completely figured out.

Many questions remain. The evolution of humans, however, is today one of the best-documented evidence of evolution's empowering force, whereas it was previously an unnerving conjecture in Darwin's grand theory. We humans are strange creatures. We have supersized brains, can stand upright on two legs, design tools to fill every want and need, speak through symbols and traditions, and have conquered every corner of the planet. Scientists have been attempting to explain how humans came to be and our role in the natural world for centuries. The vibrant setting of this story is influenced by adaptation, survival, innovation, creativity and mortality. If we could travel back in time, we could find common ancestors between ourselves and every other living organism. We could find prehistoric humans, who were curious, inventive, passionate, emotional and power hungry. Nobody, least of all the first humans, had any notion that their descendants would one day reach the moon, split the atom, achieve and master flight, build electrical gadgets, fathom the genetic code, form languages, and write history. Questions like "When did speech evolve?" and "Why did the Neanderthals become extinct?" are just a few of the many that need to be answered.

Paleoanthropology

"Evolution is written on the wings of butterflies" - Charles Darwin.

After his travels, in 1959 Charles Darwin published one of the most important scientific research ever written. *On the Origin of Species* stunned Victorian readers and revolutionized society's understanding of the full natural world. Darwin challenged Victorian doctrine by claiming that species were not eternal and that God had individually created each one. Rather life on Earth, in all its dazzling variety, had evolved through descent from a common ancestor with modification by means of natural selection. But for all of Darwin's brilliant insights into the origins of ants and armadillos, bats and barnacles, his own species is glaringly absent from the classic novel.

Of *Homo sapiens*, Darwin made only a passing mention on the third-to-last page of the tome, noting coyly that "light will be thrown on the origin of man and his history." Which is definitely still a work in progress. Which left little to nothing to conclude on Darwin's view on human evolution. That's it. That is all he wrote on the dawning of the single most consequential species on the planet. It had almost nothing on how evolution applied to humans. Darwin was determined to steer clear of the subject of human evolution because he thought it was "surrounded with prejudices."

The scientific study that covers human evolution is Paleoanthropology. Paleoanthropology is the study of human evolution through fossils, archaeological records, and extinct primates. Of colossal interest to this field is the rhythm and pattern of evolution, or the quest for the "missing link" between the great apes and humans. But is there really a "missing link"?

Paleoanthropology is a branch of anthropology, the study of human culture, society, and science. Understanding the genetic, physical, and behavioral similarities and differences between human beings and other organisms is an important part of the discipline. Paleoanthropologists search for the roots of human behavior and physical characteristics. There are so many remarkable subjects and disciplines involved with reconstruction . They are seeking to understand how evolution has influenced everyone's potentials, qualities, and restraints.

Because it looks into the evolution of our species' unique traits across millions of years, paleoanthropology is viewed by many as an intriguing branch of science. The idea of human evolution, however, might seem to clash with religious and other traditional views about how humans, other living things, and the universe came into being, which is why some people find it troubling. Nevertheless, a lot of people have learned to balance their views with the available scientific data.

Human pasts are being revealed through the investigation of relics and other symbols of human survival. Paleoanthropologists and archaeologists are grappling with each new piece of evidence. The most notable clues of this ancient history can be found in primitive human fossils and archaeological artifacts. These vestiges include bones, tools, and any other traces that earlier humans may have left behind, such as footprints, signs of hearths, or butcher scars on animal bones. The remains were often buried and preserved naturally. Then, they are unearthed either by mining underground or on the surface (exposed by rain, rivers, and wind erosion). Other crucial human qualities, such a complex and sophisticated brain, the capacity for language, and the capability to design and employ tools, came relatively recently.

Scientists can learn about the physical characteristics of human ancestors and how they changed by examining preserved bones. Bone structure, shape, and muscle marks offer information on how those ancestors walked, wielded tools. The past 100,000 years have witnessed the birth of many progressive virtues, such as dynamic symbolic expression, arts, and rich cultural diversity. Along with our ancient ancestors themselves, the account also depicts the scientists who, through discovery and discussion, piece parts of the puzzle together. A puzzle with thousands of fossil pieces and billions of DNA fragments.

By connecting together fossil tracks, scientists are learning more about our archaic forefathers behaviors, alliances, and adaptations to harsh environments. The first step—or, more precisely, the capacity to walk on two legs—was what started the eternal evolutionary path that gave rise to modern humans. About six million years ago, Sahelanthropus, one of our oldest known relatives, started the gradual transition from ape-like mobility, but Homo sapiens wouldn't appear for more than five million years. Our primate ancestors evolved from a narrow sample of sub-Saharan apes over the span of five million years to become the dominant species Homo sapiens. Africa is where humans first evolved and has been the source of much of that evolution. All early human fossils from 6 to 2 million years ago are from Africa. Between 2 million and 1.8 million years ago, the earliest members of the human race arrived in Asia from Africa. They migrated to Europe about 1.5 million and 1 million years later. Many areas of the planet were colonized by the modern human race much later. For instance, humans may have first settled in Australia just 60,000 years ago and in the Americas around 30,000 years ago. The beginnings of agriculture, cultivation and the rise of the first human civilizations date back 12,000 years. Bipedalism, or the power to move on two legs, evolved more than 4 million years ago and is one of the earliest features that distinguishes mankind. These lines of evidence increasingly indicate that *H. sapiens* originated in Africa, although not necessarily in a single time and place. Instead, it seems diverse groups of human ancestors lived in habitable regions around Africa, evolving physically and culturally in relative isolation until climate driven changes to African landscapes spurred them to intermittently mix and swap everything from genes to tool techniques. The migrations, movements, and evolution of our own species—as well as those from which we descended or with which we interbred across the ages—can be better mapped using genes than artifacts. Eventually, this process gave rise to the unique genetic makeup of modern humans.

According to Rick Potts, head of the Smithsonian's Human Origins Program, "East Africa was a setting in foment—one conducive to migrations across Africa during the period when Homo sapiens arose. It seems to have been an ideal setting for the mixing of genes from migrating populations widely spread across the continent. The implication is that the human genome arose in Africa. Everyone is African, and yet not from any one part of Africa.

Perhaps it should be a surprise, then, that when the first hominin fossil was far older and more primitive than those from Europe turned up, it came not from Africa but from Asia. The skeletons of what Dutch anatomist Eugène Dubois believed to be the long-sought missing link between apes and humans were unearthed on the Indonesian island of Java in 1891. His finding, which he dubbed Pithecanthropus erectus, spurred more efforts to establish human civilization in Asia. (We now know that Dubois' fossil belonged to Homo erectus, a hominid that was far more humanlike than apelike and lived between 700,000 and one million years ago.)

Earliest Humans

Two decades later the search turned to Europe. In 1912 amateur archaeologist Charles Dawson reported that he had found a skull with a humanlike cranium and an apelike jaw in an archaic gravel mine near the site of Piltdown in East Sussex, England. Piltdown Man, as the specimen was nicknamed, was a prime candidate for the missing link until it was exposed in 1953 as a forgery of a modern skull involving the joining of a lower jaw from an orangutan with a modern human skull.

Scholars almost completely missed a true antique hominid that popped up in Africa, one that was even older and more apelike than the one Dubois discovered, since Piltdown's claim that Europe was the cradle of humanity had seduced people. Anatomist Raymond Dart described a fossil from Taung, South Africa, with an apelike braincase and human-like molars in a paper he published in 1925, 43 years after Darwin's death. Dart gave the specimen, a young child's skull whose age is currently estimated to be around 2.8 million years old, the name Australopithecus africanus, or "the southern ape from Africa." But it would take the scientific community close to 20 years to embrace Dart's claim that the so-called Taung Child was incredibly important since the fossil traced humans to African apes.

Since then, more and more proof has accumulated that humans originated in Africa. There are already a few hominin remnants older than 2.1 million years, all of which originate from that continent.

The "Pit of Bones" in Sima de los Huesos is where the earliest early human relative's DNA has been identified. Scientists discovered tens of thousands of teeth and bones from 28 different individuals who somehow ended up being gathered collectively at the bottom of a cave in Spain's Atapuerca Mountains. The partial DNA from these 430,000-year-old remains was carefully extracted in 2016, revealing that the humans in the pit are the earliest known Neanderthals, our extremely successful and well-known near cousins. Researchers indicate that a common ancestor lived between 550,000 and 750,000 years ago based on estimates of how long it took for the distinctions between the earliest Neanderthal genome and those of modern humans to accumulate.

Although the 3.2-million-year-old ape Lucy was the first Australopithecus afarensis skeleton ever discovered, her fossil is only about 40% complete. She is considered the most famous early human ancestor in the world. Her story shines a spotlight on early human evolution and the evolution of historical science over the past 50 years. A. afarensis, discovered in 1974 by paleontologist Donald C. Johanson in Hadar, Ethiopia, was the earliest known progenitor species of humans for nearly 20 years. One of the world`s most fruitful areas for the extraction of fossils is Ethiopia's Afar Depression. This sedimentary basin, which is a part of the East African Rift System, was created by the separation of continental plates. Its sun-drenched deserts are a prime hunting ground for extinct members of the human family thanks to favorable geology.

So how did Lucy look?

Petite Lucy was three and a half feet tall with a fusion of ape and human traits, including long dangling arms and pelvis, spine, foot, and leg bones ideal for walking upright.

An apelike head with a low, heavy forehead, broadly curved cheeks, and a protruding jaw—as well as a brain around the size of a chimpanzee's—is depicted in recreations based on other A. afarensis skulls that were eventually revealed nearby.

Why was Lucy named Lucy?

Inspired by endless playings of "Lucy in the Sky With Diamonds" at a celebratory party on the day the bones were spotted, researchers gave it the Beatles' mod moniker.

How did we discover Lucy was a woman?

Lucy is clearly a girl due to her size. The size gap between male and female A. afarensis was verified by later fossil findings.

Was Lucy an adult?

There are a number of signs that Lucy is an adult. She had very human-like wisdom teeth on display, which, for starters, appeared to have been used for some time before her death, the parts of her skull that had been divided when she was a child had also grown together.

First, it illuminated one of humanity's greatest mysteries: why did our ancestors stand tall? While many of the biological features of humans and primates are similar, our bipedal locomotion is strangely unusual.

Afarensis proved that these traits did not evolve as a package, contrary to Darwin's theory that humans evolved an upright posture with stone tools, large brains and small canine teeth. Instead, upright motion was first developed before these functions.

Even when fossil discoveries proved Darwin right about the birthplace of humanity, the pattern of our emergence remained elusive. Darwin himself envisaged evolution as a phenomenon of branching in which ancestral species divide into two or more different species.However, a long-standing tradition of organizing nature according to hierarchy—dating back to Plato and Aristotle's Great Chain of Being—held hold, resulting in the conclusion that our evolution went in a linear fashion from basic to complex, primitive to sophisticated.

Researchers are sifting through ancient bone fragments and stone tools, delving into our genes, and simulating the rapidly evolving environments that helped sculpt our ancestors realms and guide their evolution in order to better understand how Homo sapiens eventually evolved from these older bloodlines of hominins, the group that comprises modern humans and our closest extinct relatives and ancestors. Human beings have evolved to be extraordinarily different in terms of physique, native tongues, and customs. How did this all come about?

Imagine someone coming into your home, taking your utensils, furniture possessions, and then burying everything in the deep woods. 12,000 years later, an archaeologist is trying to unlock your identity. What was valuable to you, what were things you enjoyed, what you believed in, and what were your influences. Because you happened to be born during a remarkable era in human history. The Planetary Revolution: when humanity transitioned, changing to be a multi-planetary species. In that time, our numbers would swell by orders of magnitude, our technology and standard of living would improve to levels previously thought unimaginable, and our self conception would transform forever. And all the ambitious archaeologist needs to know about is your rubbish in the woods. While we can only hope this will be someone's problem in 12,000 years, we have the same problem today. We're trying to reconstruct a revolution that took place 12,000 years ago. The humans who experienced the distant past as their present are now nothing beyond shadows. We can look at our world today, in crispy 4k, in color and sound. We were living in a world of black and white just three generations ago. One more generation, and we see the world through photographs. Further back, paintings and text became our main way of experiencing the past. A mere 20 generations before us today, every written word had to be copied by hand, and reports became more scarce and unreliable. The first historian lived a mere 100 generations ago. One more generation, and we see the world through photographs. Further back, our main way of experiencing the past turned into paintings and literature. Before him, there were only epics and legends and deceased kings carving themselves on pieces of stone. In the past 250 generations, images had been stripped of their original essence and just remnants remained in the soil. Eventually humanity becomes invisible and fades away. Yet, we still know some things about our ancestors. Let's try to tell their stories, and what they mean to us today!

It's been an incredible run: Over the course of 7 million years, our lineage has transformed from small apes to the dominating species on the globe. Our brains have developed to be capable of feats never before accomplished on Earth and possibly in the entire universe. Why shouldn't we keep developing brains that are more powerful? It's simple to believe that we'll keep progressing and that, in a million years, we'll have enormous brains. However, scientists can't predict our future. Some people seem to believe that the advancement of technology by humans has caused us to bypass or contradict evolution. Humans are constantly evolving, and continue to do so today. It takes countless generations of reproduction for evolution to even manifest itself. And it takes hundreds to thousands of years for changes in humans to become visible because they take so long to spread. But faster-evolving organisms also reproduce more often. For instance, because bacteria can reproduce each 20 minutes, scientists may observe their progress over a few days. All living things are always changing. Evolution can't be stopped.

I know this is a lot of information to process all at once, so why don't we go in chronological order to make it simpler to understand and summarize everything.

The Full Story

The story begins about 7 million years ago, when the human lineage broke off from chimpanzees and our relationship with the apes ended. A single female ape gave birth to two children. One was the ancestor of all chimpanzees we know today, and the other is our own mother. Over time a cast of about 20 early human species or hominins came to the fore. Most became extinct while some may have been ancestors to modern humans. Each of these species exhibited varying degrees of human-like physical and behavioral traits, that I've mentioned before like big brains, tool use, small teeth and bipedality. We share a common ancestor that lived 7 million years ago. These hominins fell into three major groups.

1. Early Hominins
2. Australopithecines
3. Homo Genus

Let's start with Early Hominins and go from there. We share a common ancestor that lived 7 million years ago. Humanity's earliest relatives lived between 7 and 4.4 millions years ago in Africa. Having most recently shared a common ancestor with Chimpanzees, they had many ape-like traits. This hominid lived sometime between 7 and 6 million years ago in West-Central Africa. Walking upright may have helped this species survive in diverse habitats, including forests and grasslands. However, fossils show that some were beginning to show human-like features like small canine teeth that were likely used for eating. A few species after that also showed signs of bipedalism. The long evolutionary journey that created modern humans began with a single step—or more accurately—with the ability to walk on two legs. One of our earliest-known ancestors, Sahelanthropus, began the slow transition from ape-like mobility some six million years ago, but Homo sapiens wouldn't show up for more than five million years.

During those long years, a plethora of unique human species lived, evolved and died out, intermingling and sometimes interbreeding along the way. As time went on, their bodies evolved, as did their brains and their cognitive abilities, as seen in the tools and technologies they invented. To skip forward a bit, no hominin fossils from somewhere around 5 millions years ago have been discovered yet. Fossils from a while later showed that even though hominids walked upright they were still tree climbers. But around 4 million years ago, grasped feet were lost. The next phase of hominin evolution was with primates called the Australopithecines.

They lived between 4.4 and 1.4 million years ago on the African continent. Like their ancient brethren, Australopithecines had some ape-like traits. However changes in the skull, spine and legs indicated a notable shift towards a human-like trait. Bipedal Locomotion. It was with *Australopithecus*, an early hominin who evolved in Southern and Eastern Africa also between 4 and 2 million years ago, that our ancestors took their first steps as committed bipeds. At that point, multiple hominin species were evolving simultaneously, and sometimes their ranges overlapped, so they may have met. By 3 million years, Hominins were living in Southern Africa.

Now, we're in the third and current phase of human evolution, involving the genus Homo, which started two million years ago. Members of the genus Homo, which in Latin means "knowing man," are a species of human. When we, Homo Sapiens, came into existence 200,000 years ago, there were at least six other human species around. Although they have found some of the first humans, scientists are still unsure of when or how the first ones developed. But unlike earlier hominids who exhibited a beautiful mosaic of ape and human traits, the homo species was becoming distinctly more human. This mosaic pattern of hominin evolution in which different body parts evolved at different rates produced some surprising creatures. For instance, *Australopithecus sediba* from South Africa, dated to 1.98 million years ago, had a humanlike hand attached to an apelike arm, a big birth canal but a small brain, and an advanced ankle bone connected to a primitive heel bone. Researchers have discovered evidence of these primitive people as well as an enigmatic "super archaic" population that split off from other humans in Africa some two million years ago. According to a report published in Science Advances in February 2020, these super archaic humans crossbred with the descendants of Neanderthals and Denisovans, other members of the Homo Genus. This is the oldest recorded occurrence of human groups mating together, however we know this occurred far more frequently in the past.

While an amount of over 20 hominin species have walked the earth, only one remains. Us. Homo Sapiens, our minds and our bodies shaped by years of evolution embarked on an explosive journey of exploration, industry, agriculture and civilization that our ancestors could have only dreamed up. Setting the world stage up for one species unprecedented rise.

Our Latter Years

Humans tend to think of themselves as apart from other animals, sort of like orphans, no family, no cousins, no parents and no living relatives. But of course, we know that isn't true. We have quite an abundance of uncivilized and uncultured cousins, once upon a time we had even more family. Living with cousins that were akin to you in intelligence and ability must have been terrifying, like living with aliens. Some lived incredibly long lives; Homo Erectus, for instance, lived for 2 million years. Ten times as long as the present-day human race. Around 10,000 years ago, the last of the other humans vanished. We don't know what led to their extinction. There was some hybridization, but not nearly enough to result in the merger of other species. Modern people carry at least a small percentage of neanderthal and other human DNA. So, we don't know if our cousins disappeared as a result of a series of modest genocides or because they lost the battle over resources. Either way, only we remain. Back to the beginnings of humanity. Early humans began using tools about 2.8 million years ago, but they didn't make much progress for almost 2 million years. Up until the advent of fire. Fire meant cooking, which increased food's nutritional value and helped our brains develop.

It also produced light and warmth, which made days longer and reduced the gloom of winter. In addition, it not only scared predators away, it could also be useful for hunting and foraging. Small animals, roasted nuts, and pre-roasted tubers were accessible from a torched wood or grassland.

Early humans were hunters and gatherers during the Paleolithic period (approximately 2.5 million years ago to 10,000 B.C.). They lived in caves, rudimentary huts, or tepees. For hunting wild animals and birds, they fashioned elementary stone and bone tools as well as crude stone axes. They harnessed controlled fire to cook their prey, which included wooly mammoths, deer, and bison. Additionally, they hunted and extracted berries, fruit, and nuts.

Paleolithic humans were the first to craft and preserve works of art. They etched humans, animals, and symbols using concoctions of minerals, ochres, roasted bone meal, and charcoal coupled with water, animal fats, and tree sap. Furthermore, they created miniature sculptures out of bones, clay, antlers, and stones.

A vast number of large mammals went extinct at the end of this era, and rising sea levels and climate change ultimately forced man to migrate as a result.

From 300,000 years ago, most of the different human species lived in small hunter-gatherer societies. They planned for the future, buried their dead, harnessed flame, timber, and stone tools, and had distinct cultures. But most importantly, they exchanged words. Most likely in a simpler kind of proto-language than our own. Could we raise some of these archaic infants today without anyone noticing that they're different? Anatomically, modern humans appeared 200,000 years ago, but probably 70,000 years is as far as we could travel back and still snatch a behaviorally modern human.

The look and manners of these people suggest that they were modern. They were much more successful with survival and explored the entire planet in a relatively short amount of time as a function of their more cooperative nature. Evidence shows that the earliest waves of humans to move out of Africa didn't have too much success on their voyages. Sometimes it seemed as though they were on the dangerous cliff of extinction, dwindling to modest numbers of 10,000." A "nuclear winter" and the following 1,000-year ice age may have resulted from Mount Toba, a supervolcano in Sumatra, erupting 70,000 years ago. An event like that would have put humans underneath a great deal of strain. Human companionship may have been the only way they were capable of survival in these intense circumstances. These archaic men and women left their homeland to journey through and settle vast areas of North Africa, Europe and Asia.

Since survival in the snowy forests of northern Europe required different traits than those needed to stay alive in Indonesia's steaming jungles, human populations evolved in different directions. Like I stated before, human evolution is messy. As a result, it's possible that tribes were constructed, and certain modern human traits, including cooperation, were acquired. Another wave of human migration left Africa between 80,000 and 50,000 years ago. At some point, around 50,000 years ago, there was an explosion in innovation. At this point, humans had a multipurpose brain and a more refined language to convey information with one another smoothly and down to the smallest detail, which led to the development of more sophisticated tools, weaponry and a more complex civilization. This allowed much closer cooperation and is what really makes us special in comparison to any other creature on Earth. Not our comparatively weak bodies and inferior senses, but the ability to cooperate flexibly in large groups, unlike for example, rigid beehives or close-knit wolf packs.

They would have encountered older, more primitive people along the way, eventually wiping them out. Before that, babies would probably lack a few crucial gene mutations. As our brain evolved, we became able to do something, life hadn't been able to do up to this point.

Building a skyscraper without knowing what a house is...is hard. But while it is easy to be arrogant in our attitude towards our ancestors, this would be ignorant. Humans 50,000 years ago were survival specialists. They had a detailed mental map of their territory, their senses were fine tuned to their environment, they knew and memorized a great amount of information about plants and animals.

They could make complicated tools that required years of careful training and very fine motor skills. Their bodies compared to our athletes today just because of their daily routines, and they lived such a rich social life within their tribe. Survival required so many skills that the average brain volume of early modern humans might even have been bigger than it is today.

It was around 20,000 years, or 800 generations ago that behaviorally modern humans began a process that would change our lifestyles forever. At first, gradually, for some of us. Then faster for more of us. And then suddenly for all of us. Back then, there were about 1 million modern humans on earth. Most other human species had died out, probably with a little help from us. Our ancestors' biology gave them the necessary tools: A general intelligence to understand things, a social intelligence to understand each other, and language to express abstract ideas and create new concepts.

These people were just like you. They suffered and experienced joy, were bored, laughed and cried. They lived in communities of a few dozen people. They controlled fire and had tools made from wood, stone and bone, told stories, mourned their dead and created art. They traded with other tribes, from obsidian to shellfish. Some hunted big game and were very mobile, and others relied more on plants they collected, and others mostly stayed in one area with an abundance of seafood. This was the common state of humanity for most of history. Until a slow transition, step by step, turned into a revolution.

Earth's beginnings can be traced back 4.5 billion years, but human evolution only counts for a tiny speck of its history. The Prehistoric Period—or when there was human life before records documented human activity—roughly dates from 2.5 million years ago to 1,200 B.C. It is generally categorized in three archaeological periods: the Stone Age, Bronze Age, and Iron Age.

From the invention of tools made for hunting to advances in food production and agriculture to early examples of art and religion, this enormous time span—ending roughly 3,200 years ago (dates vary upon region)—was a period of great transformation. Here's a closer look:

The first solid evidence for this stems from the Jordan Valley, where our ancestors collected wild wheat more than 20,000 years ago. They noticed that seeds in the ground made more plants the next year. If they put the good ones in one place, next year they had more of the good ones. This was a great supplement to hunting and gathering. You could prepare some crops, return next year, build a temporary settlement and have a secure food supply. Our ancestors used these bonus crops to bake the first bread and to brew the first beer. With every generation, they gained deeper knowledge about the plants and animals around them and how to manipulate them to their advantage. But there was a lot to learn. Very slowly, from generation to generation, pockets of knowledge expanded and were passed along, to be expanded again.

But then around 12,000 years ago, in multiple locations, humans developed agriculture. Everything changed very quickly. Before, survival as a hunter and forager required superb physical and mental abilities in all fields, from everybody. Most of the calories we consume today stem from about 15 different founder crops that humans began to domesticate in earnest in the next few thousand years. With the rise of the agricultural age, individuals could increasingly rely on the skills of others for survival. This meant some of them could specialize. Maybe they worked on better tools, maybe they took more time to breed resistant livestock, maybe they started inventing things.

The first temple was also built 12,000 years ago. Hundreds of humans gathered in the hills of Southern Anatolia. They were hunters and gatherers without the knowledge of agriculture or metalworking. All they had were tools made of stone and wood, but they built humanity's first big construction project. 7,000 years before the pyramids were built in Egypt. Spread over 300 meters, our ancestors erected circles of massive stone pillars. Decorated with art for pictograms and stone carvings of animals and mythical creatures. We have no idea how they were able to do this. It was probably a project of epic scale for the Stone Age, requiring a level of organization we didn't know early humans were capable of until we found this site. So why did they build it? The most popular theory is that this was the first temple of humanity dedicated to long-forgotten gods. We only know that this construction project, the 1st of its kind, marks the beginning of a new era. It's around this time that humans truly began to build their own world. This moment in time is so distinct that scientist Cesare Emiliani proposed that humanity should switch to the Holocene calendar, by adding 10,000 years to our Gregorian calendar.

As farming got more and more efficient, what we call civilization began. Agriculture gave us a reliable and predictable food source, which allowed humans to hoard food on a large scale for the first time, which is much easier to do with grains than meat. The food stock needed protection, which led to communities living together in tighter spaces.

It took nearly a millennium until Jericho, probably the first city on Earth, was founded after the start of the human era. Over the next thousand years, more and more permanent settlements appeared around the world, and more and more plants and animals were domesticated as agriculture spread. Evidence for trade over thousands of kilometers has been found from this period. Around 5,000,000 humans were alive at this point in history. Technology advanced constantly at a slow pace. Pottery became widespread. The first cultural communities appeared in China, India and the Fertile Crescent. Around 8,000 years ago from today, humans started to use metal for the first time, learning to use tin and copper and kickstarting what we know as the Bronze age. The first proto writing emerged and the wheel was invented. In South America, the Chinchorro culture started to artificially mummify humans 2,000 years earlier than in ancient Egypt. The first high cultures also started emerging.

- The Indus Valley Civilization
- Ancient Egypt
- The Minoans in Greece
- And the Sumerians in Mesopotamia

During the Bronze Age, metalworking advances were made, as bronze, a copper and tin alloy, was discovered. Now used for weapons and tools, the harder metal replaced its stone predecessors, and helped spark innovations including the ox-drawn plow and the wheel.

This time period also brought advances in architecture and art, including the invention of the potter's wheel, and textiles—clothing consisted of mostly wool items such as skirts, kilts, tunics and cloaks. Home dwellings morphed to so-called roundhouses, consisting of a circular stone wall with a thatched or turf roof, complete with a fireplace or hearth, and more villages and cities began to form.

Organized government, law and warfare, as well as beginnings of religion, also came into play during the Bronze Age, perhaps most notably relating to the ancient Egyptians who built the pyramids during this time. The earliest written accounts, including Egyptian hieroglyphs and petroglyphs (rock engravings), are also dated to this era.

Stonehenge was built in Britain, and the first dynasty in China began. What we consider history now started and things started picking up pace, as the world population continued to rise.

A number of new, high cultures appeared, many writing down their legends. More and more cities were founded. In South America, the Olmec culture emerged. Around this time, the legendary siege of Troy is supposed to have happened. Soon after in the Easter Mediterranean in the Fertile Crescent, the Bronze Age ended in violence. Every Bronze Age culture, except Egypt, was destroyed by mysterious invaders. Writing and progress froze for hundreds of years.

Years later, what we consider Western culture began. The Greek City states beat off the Persian invasion, and triggered their golden era, ended by Alexander the Great around 200 years later. 100 years later, Rome destroyed Carthage, and became a dominant force in the world. Caesar was murdered 156 years later, while the world population had risen to about 300,000,000 people. As we reach the end of that century, we've reached the point where the Gregorian calendar and our current method of marking human history begins. A mere 2,000 years from now, humans will walk on the moon.

First, early defense structures were built, the need for organization grew. The more organized we got, the faster things became efficient. Villages became cities, cities became kingdoms, kingdoms became empires. Connections between humans exploded, which led to opportunities to exchange knowledge. Progress became exponential. About 500 years ago, the scientific revolution began. Mathematics, Physics, Astronomy and Biology transformed everything we thought we knew. The Industrial Revolution followed soon after, laying the foundation for the modern world. As our overall efficiency grew exponentially, more people could spend their lifetime contributing to the overall progress of humanity. Revolutions kept happening. The invention of the computer, its evolution into a medium we all use on a daily basis, and the rise of the internet shaped our world. It's hard to grasp how fast all that happened. It's been about 125,000 generations since the emergence of the first human species. About 7,500 generations since the physiologically modern humans saw the light of day. 500 generations ago, what we call civilization began. 20 generations ago, we learned how to do science. And the internet became available to most people only one generation ago.

If we think about it, as a building project that started 12,000 years ago when for the first time, our ancestors came together to carve a temple out of bedrock with tools made of stone; not knowing what they would set in motion, and where it would lead us as a species. From building the first temple, to ships flying beyond the sky. Today, we live in the most prosperous age humanity has ever experienced.

We've transformed this planet, from the composition of its atmosphere to large-scale changes in the landscape, and also in terms of the other animals in existence. We light up the night, with artificial stars and put people in a metal box in the sky, we've walked robots on other planets. We looked deep into the past of our universe with mechanical eyes. Our knowledge and our way of storing more of it is exploding. The average high school student today knows more about the universe than a scholar a few centuries ago. Humans dominate this planet, even if our rule is very fragile.

We're still not that different from our ancestors, 700,000 years ago. But our lifestyle has existed for less than 0.001% of human history. Just contemplate the remarkable achievements we have accomplished in such a short period of time, and the harm we have brought to the planet as well. From here on, there's no saying what the future holds for us. We're building a skyscraper, but we're not sure if it's standing on a solid foundation or if we're building it on quicksand.

Don't miss out!

Visit the website below and you can sign up to receive emails whenever Vaishali Alapati publishes a new book. There's no charge and no obligation.

https://books2read.com/r/B-A-MMRV-WCEDC

BOOKS2READ

Connecting independent readers to independent writers.

Did you love *The Humans Lost in Time*? Then you should read *The Full History of Evolutionary Thought*[1] by Vaishali Alapati!

[2]

The emergence of evolutionary theory has an illustrious history. It transcends several eras, is rich with a cornucopia of ideas, and is a fusion of logic, philosophy, ethics, and raw curiosity. Written history chronicles the merits of each individual, from Anaximander, who recognized the germs of a marvelous theory, to Gregor Mendel, whose research completed Darwin's theory of evolution. This volume recounts the colorful history of evolutionary thought, and documents all the perspectives that came into play.

---

1. https://books2read.com/u/4AveAd

2. https://books2read.com/u/4AveAd

Also by Vaishali Alapati

Evolution Unraveled
History of Evolutionary Thought: Part 1
History of Evolutionary Thought: Part 2
"Dark-DNA"
Epigenetics 101
The Full History of Evolutionary Thought
The Humans Lost in Time